8/15

THE RIGHT WORDS FOR ANY OCCASION

new seasons®

Contributing writers:
Valorie Lorraine Cason, Susan J. Letham, Jennifer John Ouellette,
Kathryne Lee Tirrell, and Lynda Twardowski

New Seasons is a registered trademark of Publications International, Ltd.

Louis Weber, CEO
Publications International, Ltd.
7373 North Cicero Avenue
Lincolnwood, Illinois 60712

www.pilbooks.com

Permission is never granted for commercial purposes.

Manufactured in China.

8 7 6 5 4 3 2 1

ISBN-13: 978-1-4127-0612-4
ISBN-10: 1-4127-0612-2

Contents

The Right Words...Right Now

Staying in touch with the important people in our lives is a rewarding but challenging task. Busy, busy, busy. Rush, rush, rush. It's too easy to lose track of the people you care about. Remember when you were a kid? You and your best friend tied two tin cans together with a string, then stretched it tight. The right words are like that string: They keep you connected to loved ones.

For many people, the thought of expressing feelings and emotions on paper is downright daunting. But it doesn't need to be! After all, the words themselves are not nearly as important as the thought behind them. Your thoughtfulness takes the most simple sentiments and turns them into gestures of kindness and gratitude, love and celebration, sympathy and support. Your thoughtfulness reaches out to the people you care about and reminds them that they are in your thoughts, your heart, and even your prayers. Let *The Right Words for Any Occasion* act as a gentle reminder that the most important words are not the fanciest—or even necessarily spelled correctly—but are those words that are most heartfelt.

To add a finishing touch to your card, you may want to include a small but thoughtful gift. It doesn't need to be a monetary gift—small items like bookmarks or sachets, or stickers and gum for children, can make opening a card a memorable experience. (Don't forget to add appropriate postage if you include an "extra" in your card.)

It is our hope that the simple expressions in this book will inspire you to create and keep connections with the people you care about. Pick up a pen, choose a blank card, keep it simple, and remember that anything that comes from your heart is bound to be beautiful.

Birthday Wishes

Everybody wants to be treated like a king or queen on their birthday. The perfect words will make anyone's birthday a celebration fit for royalty.

Happy Birthday

~

You know those memories that make you laugh out loud? I hope you make many new ones today.
Happy birthday!

~

Enjoy all the love and affection that comes your way today. You deserve it!

~

Hoping your birthday is wrapped in smiles.

~

Your loving heart brightens the lives of all who know you. May this be your happiest birthday ever.

The importance of birthdays is not how many you've had but rather how well you've celebrated.

~

Birthdays are a day for reflection . . . to celebrate who you are and who you will become.

~

Pleasant thoughts
are sent your way
with a heartfelt wish
for a happy day.

~

I can't imagine my world without you.
Happy birthday.

Savor each day for the gift that it is.

May you delight in the simple treasures of life on your birthday.

The secret of a happy life is to think kindly of the past and live fully in the now. Have a wonderful birthday.

Hoping your day is a keepsake to hold in your heart.

Hoping happy dreams and magical moments surround you on your special day.

May your birthday make you feel as beautiful and special as you are.

May love, laughter, and contentment decorate your day and fill your year.

Heartfelt wishes for a memorable birthday.

May the joy you give to others come back to you today.

Another birthday, another year of memories. Let's celebrate!

There are exactly 86,400 seconds in your birthday. Enjoy every one!

Special People

~

I am so proud to have a son who does so much, for so many. You deserve the happiest of birthdays.

~

This is a wonderful day, and you're a wonderful daughter. Happy birthday.

~

It's a one-of-a-kind day for a one-of-a-kind granddaughter. Hope this birthday is as special as you are!

~

Grandson, you bring excitement and a feeling of youth to everyone around you. Here's to another year of fantastic adventures!

~

This is a day to celebrate your life and everything you mean to us! Happy birthday, Dad.

You never ran out of time, pride, laughter, or love. Have a great birthday, Dad.

~

Mom, your birthday is the perfect time for us to remind you how much we love you.

~

You've given me the greatest gifts a child can receive—love, laughter, and kindness. Today I give them back to you. Happy birthday, Mom!

~

Happy birthday to a grandfather who shines with happiness and so readily shares it. May your day be as happy as you make others.

~

Grandmother, you touch the lives and hearts of everyone you meet. Happy birthday to a woman who means so much to so many!

Your love has passed from heart to heart across the generations. Happy birthday, Grandma!

Grandmas are like birthday cake—soft, sweet, and the best thing in the house! Hope your day is as wonderful as you, Grandma!

Special Years

Sweet 16—it's the first step toward your grown-up life! Happy birthday.

Rev up the engine and give this celebration some gas—you've got a license to party! Happy 16th birthday!

May your adventures today be as fun as you are! Happy 21st birthday.

Congratulations on passing the last hurdle to officially become an adult! Happy 21st birthday.

Thirty years of practice has certainly paid off! You look great!

Wishing you laughter and happiness today and every day. Happy 30th birthday.

May your next 50 years be as fantastic as the first! Happy birthday!

Wishing for you a day that holds all the happiness your heart can imagine. Happy 50th birthday.

Child's Birthday

What makes today so extraordinary?
It isn't ice cream, cake, candles, or
presents—it's you!

Wish on a star, walk on a moonbeam,
dance on a rainbow—today was made
for miracles like you.

The birthday fairy
has come to say,
have a wonderful time
on your special day!

With each new year you bring more
cheer. Happy birthday to a great kid.

Go ahead, make a wish. You're proof
they do come true. Happy birthday!

I wish you magic and laughter
and everything else that you're after.
Happy birthday.

Remember the day you were born?
I do—and that's why I'm celebrating
today!

We just want to tell you
how treasured you are,
and how much we love you,
our own little star.
Happy birthday!

Congratulations!

Success may be the easiest of all occasions to write about. Imagine your fondest dream has come true. Now write to that special person the words you'd like to hear.

General Congratulations

It's true—good things *do* happen to great people!

Celebrating success! Celebrating YOU! Congratulations.

You are proof that dreams and possibilities are endless when you believe in yourself.

Bells! Whistles! Fireworks! Well done!

Lucky you! I'm so happy for you.

Enjoy the love, laughter, and limelight that is yours today.

Envisioning a dream is easy. Seeing it through is not! Congratulations.

Thank you for letting me share your joy! Happiness shared is delight doubled.

I'm overjoyed! It couldn't have happened to a nicer person.

Three cheers from me to you on your triumphant day!

I'm so happy for you. You deserve nothing but the best.

～

No one deserves success more than you. Congratulations!

～

Whatever you've been doing, keep doing it!

～

Isn't it great when everything comes up roses?

～

I hope this is just the first of many good things to come!

～

Congratulations! Your joy has brightened my life, too.

～

Your good news makes my heart sing. Congratulations!

You did it! I rejoice with you in your triumph.

～

I'm delighted about your news! You truly earned this success.

～

You deserve a round of applause for a job well done!

～

May the happiness you're feeling today go on and on and on!

Graduation

～

May all paths lead to happiness, and may all your dreams come true.

～

We may have different talents and dreams, but we each have the power to shape our future. Congratulations!

Congratulations on your graduation! Always be proud of your achievements, and use them to fulfill your dreams.

I've watched you climb the ranks to where you are today, and I never doubted for a second that you would make it all the way. Congratulations.

Wishing you adventure, success, and happiness for all your tomorrows.

Your brilliant mind is honed for success. Congratulations!

May I make an educated guess? You're the brightest and the best! Happy graduation!

Congratulations. What an outstanding achievement!

We are so proud of all your accomplishments—in the past and, especially, today.

Look boldly into the future and be confident as you walk your life's path.

For all the successes behind you, I send congratulations. For all the challenges ahead, I send blessings.

Congratulations on your monumental achievement.

Graduation is just one day, but it reaps rewards that last a lifetime.

~

Wishing you success and smiles on your graduation and always.

~

Hold tight to the dreams you have today, and walk boldly in their direction.

~

I'm so proud of you and all you've achieved. Congratulations on your graduation.

~

Stay committed to your dreams and they, too, will become reality.

~

You have every right to be proud of your achievements. Have a great graduation day!

Ready for success? Then set out into your new life and meet it halfway.

~

Commencement means a new beginning. May the memories you've already made inspire an unforgettable future.

~

A cap. A gown. A diploma. A whole new chapter in the story of you. Congratulations.

~

I'm so pleased for you! Now it's time to show the world how you shine!

~

Happy graduation! Today marks the end of your formal education but only the beginning of a lifetime of discovery.

You're intelligent, determined, and ready to change the world. Congratulations on your graduation.

~

You've studied hard and worked hard. Today, take it easy! Happy graduation.

~

Give yourself credit for your successes. Stand tall and proud on your special day.

~

One last lesson as you prepare for the world: Always be true to yourself.

Engagement

~

What greater joy can there be for two souls than to know they are destined to be together? Congratulations on your engagement.

May this be the first of endless expressions of your love for one another.

~

I'm so glad to hear that you're tying the knot! Congratulations.

~

Sparkling stone, sparkling future. Congratulations.

~

Life looks kindly on those who love and bestows special blessings on those who join their hearts.

~

Here comes the bride! Happy engagement!

Congratulations! ❦ 19

From sneaking kisses
to wedding wishes!
Congratulations.

~

Congratulations. How wonderful that
you've found your soul mate.

~

May today be the beginning of a
lifetime of beautiful days.

~

Milk and cookies.
Toast and jam.
You two.
Some things are just better together!

Expecting a Baby

~

I heard you've got a special delivery on
the way—congratulations!

How wonderful that you're adding
more love to the world.

~

May your new baby bless your life with
joy and happiness. Congratulations!

~

Your baby is very lucky: What better
parents than you!

~

A few months from now you'll learn
that you *can* do three things at once
and that moms really *do* have eyes in
the back of their heads.

~

Take care of yourself, and let God do
the rest. Congratulations on your
miracle from above.

~

Babies are little miracles with a whole
lot of "kick." Congratulations on your
pregnancy.

May you savor the sweet joys of parenthood.

Wishing you a happy, healthy bundle of love!

A baby is God's way of telling us hope is alive and well.

New Job

You're a success looking for a chance to happen! Congratulations on your new job.

You've always been one step above the rest. Good luck with your promotion.

A new job, new friends, new challenges—good luck!

I always knew you'd go far—clearly, I'm not the only one to recognize this! Congratulations on your new job!

There's no limit to what you can achieve! Good luck in your new position.

Congratulations on your new job. It couldn't have happened to a better person!

I never doubted that you would race up the corporate ladder. I'm so happy for you.

Attitude, intelligence, determination. You've got it all—and now you've got the job to prove it. Congratulations!

To many more years of successful dividends!

～

Congratulations on your latest step up the ladder of success.

New Home

～

May the sun always shine brightly through your windows. Congratulations on your new home.

～

May your new house be home to harmony, peace, and love.

～

May you feel safe and snug in your new home!

～

May your new home hold the key that unlocks your dreams.

It's true, there's no place like home. I'm glad you've found a nice one!

～

A home is like an old friend—it's always there to hold and comfort you. Congratulations on your new home.

～

Home is where the heart makes its memories. Wishing you all the best in your new house.

～

Wishing you a home filled with the love of your family and the laughter of your friends.

～

New friends await
wherever you roam—
I'm happy to hear
that you've found a new home.

Welcome to your new home. May it be the foundation of many happy memories.

~

May you enjoy quiet moments and peaceful hours in your new home.

Retirement

~

You've helped your family grow and prosper, now it's time to relax and enjoy the results.

~

It's time to live life according to your own schedule; savor every minute of it! Congratulations.

~

Now it's time to REALLY work— work hard at enjoying life, that is. Congratulations.

Time to enjoy the harvest. Happy retirement!

~

Rest. Relax. Rejuvenate. Congratulations on your retirement.

~

Enjoy every minute of your retirement—you earned them all!

~

If life has a "best time," then this is it! Congratulations on your retirement.

~

Late nights, lazy mornings, long lunches … love it! Happy retirement!

~

What's so great about retirement? Everything!

~

No starting time. No quitting time. It's about time!

Saying Thanks

Gratitude is easy to express if you just pick up that pen and tell someone exactly how their gift or thoughtful action made you feel.

Friends like you are a rare treasure. Thank you for all you've done.

~

May life bring you a reflection of the kindness you've shown to others. Thank you for your thoughtfulness.

~

Thanks for all you've done for me. Next time, it's my turn.

Just saying thank you because you've been thoughtful so often!

~

May you be blessed for the kindness you've shown me.

~

A kind deed is like water for a flower: It makes the heart bloom. Thanks for planting a garden in my heart.

~

My "thank you" seems so small compared to all you've done, but it comes from my heart.

Your kind gesture will last a lifetime. Thank you.

I was praying for a miracle, and then you came along.

Your thoughtful gift brought a smile to my face. Thank you!

One person. One deed. A million thanks.

You are a gift to my life. Thanks for everything.

Knowing you're there to cheer me on is making things so much easier. Thank you!

I'm overwhelmed by your generosity. Thank you so much!

Only you could have known exactly what would make my day. Thank you for knowing me better than I know myself.

For one person, you do an awful lot of good. Thanks.

It's a comfort to know we can count on each other through whatever life brings. Thanks.

How did a person like me get lucky
enough to have a friend like you?
Thanks for all you've done.

May your thoughtfulness find its way
back to you.

You have a special gift for listening
with your heart. Thank you.

A good deed is a reflection of a
person's soul. You are beautiful.
Thank you.

Thanks for helping me make
molehills out of my mountains.
What would I do without you?

You always brighten my day. I'm so
grateful.

Your giving nature and unselfish ways
are a blessing to everyone who knows
you. Thank you.

Some people give hugs. Some people
give help. You gave your all. Thanks.

I'm better…because you're the best.
Thank you.

Generosity is a sign of a great soul.
You're surely one. Thank you for
everything.

You've restored my faith. I'll be
forever thankful.

Your kindness touched my heart.
Thank you.

The way you come to the aid of others is fabulous. You are a treasure. Thank you.

There are no words to express my gratitude for all you've done. Thank you so much.

I'll always remember your kindness. Thank you very much.

Kind deeds change lives. Thank you.

Sometimes simple words say it best. Thank you from the bottom of my heart.

A person like you brightens the world for the rest of us. Thank you!

You have a "gift for giving"! Thank you so much.

Thank you—for what you did, what you said, and who you are.

I will always be grateful to you for your thoughtfulness and consideration. Thank you.

Sympathy

Sometimes bad things happen to people you love. It's hard to know what to say to help, but your caring words can make a difference.

Condolence

When your heart is empty, filling it with happy memories can help.

It's hard to understand why people are taken from us, but find comfort in knowing you were a special part of a well-lived life.

If I can help you at this time of sadness, I'm here.

Take heart. Time will soften the edges and ease your burden.

Memories of love and friendship are treasures to carry with you always.

My heart aches for you. I'm sorry for your loss.

Love follows us, no matter how far.

When the Lord calls our loved ones home, he leaves a gift of memories in exchange. I'm here if you want to talk.

Hold on to your memories, and let them guide you during this time of sadness.

God is always in your corner at a time like this—and so am I.

I was saddened to hear of your loss. Please know how very sorry I am.

You're in my thoughts every step of the way.

We hold you safe in our hearts at this time of sadness.

Sorrow is a fleeting emotion, but love is infinite.

I cannot take away your pain, but I can listen if you want to talk about it.

Take comfort—those who love will be reunited in eternity.

Memories are the legacy of love.

Magic happens when two hearts become connected, and memories can never be erased. I'm so sorry for your loss.

She (He) is not alone . . . and neither are you.

You need not feel alone. Just say the word and I'll be there.

Have hope in tomorrow, have faith in the everlasting, and take comfort in the love of friends and family.

With deep sympathy from your friends at this time of sadness.

Time and prayer are the keys to healing pain. I offer you both.

God gave us shoulders for a reason. Lean on me.

We cannot feel life's losses without first feeling the blessings of its fullness.

If you need a friend to hold you, my arms are open.

May God's love make your grief bearable.

May happy memories carry you through this sorrowful time.

You're in my thoughts, my heart, and my prayers.

Wishing you and your family strength and peace.

May hope find its way to your heart.

Where answers fail, seek prayer.
Find peace.

May angels walk with you today and
always.

Divorce

Take the lessons you've learned and
the love you shared, and turn it into
knowledge for tomorrow.

Take comfort in having made the
right choice, and take comfort in your
friends. We're here when you need us.

Getting a divorce is devastating, but
not as disastrous as spending your
life with the wrong person. I'm here if
you need me.

The toughest moments in life don't
break us—they make us.

Time can heal a broken heart, but you
have to surrender the pieces. I'm here
if you need me.

Loss is really the hand of fortune
leading us onward to better things.

No matter how alone you feel, you're
not. I'm here for you.

Look within, find strength. Look around, find me.

You will get through this. I know, because I know you.

Don't dwell too long on what was or what might have been; what will be is waiting.

Angels hover close to those whose hearts are breaking.

Beyond the pain, opportunity awaits. I promise.

May the love and support of your friends and family carry you past this difficult time.

Look at the silver lining—this is a chance to move on and fulfill higher hopes, better goals, and greater challenges.

Take this time to regroup, refocus, and aim higher.

Sometimes you have to get lost to find your true direction.

This is not just a setback, it's a setup for a better opportunity.

⁓

This is a wonderful chance to find out "What would happen if…?"

⁓

Don't fear the challenges that lie ahead; I'm right beside you.

⁓

If laughter is the best medicine… laugh at those stuck in rush hour traffic! I know you'll be on the road to success again soon.

⁓

These times are uncertain, but one thing's for sure: I'm here for you.

⁓

Often the greatest journeys in life are those that weren't on the itinerary.

Bad things happen to good people because they have the strength to overcome. I'm here if you need me.

General Encouragement

⁓

ALWAYS know you're NEVER alone.

⁓

I hope it lightens your burden to know I'm here for you.

⁓

I'm proud of how well you're coping.

⁓

It takes a little darkness for us to see the stars, and a whole lifetime to reach them. Don't give up.

⁓

I hope you'll remember you have friends who will listen and care… and I'm one of them.

Don't give up. There are better times
to come.

An ear to listen
A hand to hold
A heart to share
A friend who cares.
Don't hesitate to call.

You may not feel better tomorrow,
next week, or next month, but you *will*
feel better.

Now is a good time to take a look at
your life's map, find a better route,
and move forward in the direction of
the good things in your future.

Words don't always help, so I'm
sending you loving thoughts as well.

Each day is easier than the one before.
Keep looking ahead.

I know your shining spirit will pull
you through.

Even though it's hard to see through
the darkness, try to remember you'll
come into the light a stronger person.

Thinking of You

Say a simple hello or tell a loved one how much you miss them.
Just make sure you let them know they're on your mind!

You're a Great Friend

To have a friend is to have everything.

You're like family to me. Thanks for being such a great friend.

Friendship is a privilege—I feel privileged to have you as a friend.

You touch my life in a million wonderful ways. What a great friend!

When I count my blessings, our friendship tops the list.

A friend is a guardian angel in disguise. Thanks for always watching out for me.

We've played roles in many chapters of each other's lives. Thank you for being such a true and faithful friend.

Good friends are the rare jewels of life—difficult to find and impossible to replace.

To have one true friend is lucky. To have a friend like you is a miracle.

We've known each other so long we don't always need words. Even so, I want to tell you that I cherish our friendship.

You help me keep my dreams alive. Thank you for your friendship.

My favorite moments are always spent with you. They are filled with love and topped with laughter.

I Miss You

The miles between us are nothing because you're always in my heart.

Just because you haven't heard from me lately doesn't mean you haven't been in my thoughts. I miss you.

Out of sight, out of mind? Not a chance!

We may be far apart, but you're always in my thoughts.

If wishing could make it so, you'd be here with me right now.

The echo of your laughter brightens my day—I miss you!

From the first minute of the day to the last of the night, my thoughts are filled with memories of you. I'm counting the minutes until I see you again.

Missing the good old days of you and me.

When you're not with me I just can't get it together. I miss you so much!

~

If every thought I had of you were a shining star, the night would be as bright as day. I miss you!

~

"Wish you were here" just doesn't express how much I miss you.

~

I've been thinking about you so much that I feel like we're together again.

~

Just the thought of you makes me feel closer to home.

~

You're there. I'm here. We're nuts!

~

Hold our memories in your heart, and you'll never feel alone.

I wish you were here so that when I say "Remember when...," I can actually see your smile and hear your laugh.

~

I just wanted to reach out and tell you how much I miss you.

~

Sending good old-fashioned hugs and kisses with good old-fashioned snail mail.

~

If I only had a minute with you for every time you're in my thoughts, we'd never be apart.

Keep in Touch

If absence makes the heart grow
fonder, you must be my fondest
friend! Please keep in touch.

Sharing with friends makes life much
more fun. Please write.

I just wanted to let you know I'm
thinking of you. I'd love to know how
you're doing.

Sending checkup prayers
to be sure you're okay
and wishes that
I'll hear from you today.
Keep in touch.

I'm always thinking about you. Be sure
to keep me up-to-speed on your life.

I hope you're doing well. Do tell!

Through your letters, I hear your
laughter. Please write soon.

I don't care if it's e-mail, snail mail,
phone, telegram, or smoke signal—
please keep in touch!

We may be far apart, but you're always
in my heart.

Time has a way of slipping away from us—let's hold tight to our friendship.

Although the miles between us keep us apart, there is no distance between our hearts.

Thoughts of you always make me smile.

I hope this note finds you with a happy heart.

Just thinking of you can make me happy. Thanks for being there for me even when we can't be together.

I was just counting my blessings, and you came to mind.

I wish I could reach out and hug you!

You're always in my thoughts and prayers.

May your day be filled with all the happiness it can hold.

My thoughts, my heart, and my love are with you.

I wish I could say hello in person, but since I can't, I'm hoping this will do.

Get Well Soon

A simple note with a few well-thought-out words can go a long way toward sending a loved one on the road to recovery.

May the sun shine on your speedy recovery.

Get better soon—there is still much joy ahead of you!

I'm sorry you've been under the weather. I hope you'll be feeling sunny again soon!

Sending you an express delivery of best wishes for a speedy recovery!

That was quite a scare! I'm so thankful you're feeling stronger.

Sorry to hear you've been laid up. Get well soon.

If there is anything I can do to make you feel better, I'll feel better as well.

We all miss your smile, and hope you'll feel better soon.

We miss you when you're not here. Here's wishing you a speedy recovery!

Just a little get well wish to brighten your day.

Hope you're feeling back on top of the world soon!

I hope this card will brighten your day and help you get better without delay.

Look on the bright side, at least you get breakfast in bed! Get well soon.

No worries.
No stress.
Just get some rest.
Feel better soon!

Step back and remember what's most important . . . you! Get well soon.

Keep your chin up, your temperature down, and get well soon.

While your body regains strength, let my love help sustain your spirit.

May your hospital stay be short and filled with constant love and support.

Thinking of you as you recover, and sending prayers to make you stronger. Get well soon.

Wishing you a short stay and a speedy recovery!

~

May sunshine find you in your hospital room and light the way to a full recovery.

Long Illness

~

Best wishes as you fight this illness. My prayers are with you.

~

You are in my thoughts and prayers. I hope things look brighter soon.

~

May hope and faith bring you peace during this difficult time.

You may feel like a stranger in your own skin right now. Call me, and I'll remind you of the courageous person inside.

~

The way you've handled what has been dealt to you has been so inspiring. Your spirit has shined through it all.

~

Have faith, have strength, have courage. You will beat this.

I Love You

Trust your heart. Be simple and sincere.
The feelings in your heart will show in your words.

You're forever on my mind and in my heart. I love you!

~

My heart beats BECAUSE of you. My life IS you.

~

It's amazing that love can transform your life forever. Thank you for your love.

~

I am so thankful for the gift of you.

~

Our relationship is a blessing. Please know that I love you.

Anywhere with you is a wonderful place to be.

~

Without your love, I wouldn't be the person I am today.

~

Your love is my most treasured gift.

You are never alone when you are loved. I love you.

~

I'll never grow tired of telling you how much I love you.

~

Love shared is love multiplied. I want you to know I love you.

~

Your love holds me together.

~

Life means much more to me knowing I have you to love.

~

Love is contagious.... I caught it from you.

~

I'm glad we're taking life's journey together. I love you.

Your love is a treasure that makes me rich beyond my wildest dreams.

~

I don't know where I would be without you, and I'm happy that I don't have to find out.

~

When two hearts listen, they don't need words.

~

Our love isn't a fairy tale—it's better. It's real.

~

Three little words express what you mean to me: I love you!

~

I want to spend my life with you— I love you.

The day I fell in love with you was the best day of my life.

⁓

You are my happily ever after. I love you.

⁓

You captured my heart with your very first smile and continue to amaze me with each new day. I love you.

⁓

God blessed us with a love that lasts a lifetime.

⁓

Life without you? Not a chance. Life with you? Endless romance. Thank you for your love.

⁓

Only one thing makes me happier than you: Us.

Being with you makes me feel like a kid again. I love you.

⁓

Falling in love with you was the best thing that ever happened to me.

⁓

You keep my feet on the ground and my head on my shoulders, but you make my heart soar.

With Love

Wedding Bells

A wedding is undoubtedly one of life's most joyful events. Celebrate love from the depths of your heart, and the right words are sure to follow.

May the joy of this day be yours for the rest of your lives.

⁓

May your love continue to grow stronger with each passing day.

⁓

Love and laughter. For today. Forever.

Wishing you both an eternity of wedded bliss.

⁓

It's a day you'll remember forever. Treasure it as I treasure both of you.

⁓

Let love lead the way through your life together.

⁓

May your love begin with "Once upon a time..." and end with "happily ever after." Best wishes to you both on your wedding day.

Health. Wealth. Happiness. May your life together be abundantly blessed.

~

This is the most important promise you'll ever make.

~

May the light of love cast its glow on your lives.

~

May God bless the two of you as you become one.

~

Two people. One life. From this day forward.

~

I can't imagine a nicer couple! Congratulations on your wedding day.

~

Let your love be a fire that you kindle every day.

Wishing you a marriage flavored with happiness and spiced with adventure.

~

May the love you share today grow stronger every day of your lives.

~

Two hands, two hearts, two souls... one love. May you have a beautiful wedding day!

~

I believe the sound of wedding bells rings all the way to heaven. Have a wonderful wedding day.

~

Cherish joy.
Cherish love.
Cherish each other.

~

May the exhilaration of new love remain in your hearts always.

Marriage is a communion of souls blessed by angels. Congratulations!

~

You two deserve all the love and happiness in the world.

~

Congratulations on finding your true love.

~

Enjoy love and happiness from this day forward.

You've tied the knot—may it keep your hearts bound together forever.

~

I hope the two of you will always share the caring and closeness you have today.

~

One life is a miracle, but two lives knit together is a joy beyond words.

~

God knows you're perfect for each other... and so do I!

~

May love be in every step you take, in every word you speak, and in every choice you make in your life together.

~

May your marriage be strong and blessed all the days of your lives.

Happy Anniversary

Anniversaries—your own or someone else's—are a good time to count life's blessings. Bring a smile to someone's face by reminding them how fortunate they are.

May every tomorrow be twice as sunny and sweet as all the days that came before.

May you continue to grow together in life and love.

Wishing you more love with every year you share.

My love for you grows stronger with each passing year.

The best way to enjoy life is to savor the passing of time. Let's celebrate another year together.

Your life together is an inspiration. Happy anniversary!

Celebrate the love you share.

You have a wonderful gift in each other. Happy anniversary.

The honeymoon still isn't over! Happy anniversary.

Congratulations and much love to you both on your anniversary.

May your lives continue to be blessed by love.

May you spend the rest of your lives traveling hand in hand. Happy anniversary!

~

Together we have everything we need. Happy anniversary.

~

It's hard enough to find love, but the two of you found the miracle of true love. Here's to many more beautiful years together.

~

I found compassion in your eyes, comfort in your arms, and eternal love in your heart. Happy anniversary.

Special Years

~

Our first year together has been pure bliss. I love you!

Happy first anniversary. May you know many more years of joy and love.

~

Your love is an inspiration. Happy 25th anniversary!

~

Congratulations on your silver anniversary. Your marriage was truly made in heaven.

~

Fifty years of wedded bliss, each worth its weight in gold. Congratulations on your golden anniversary.

~

May your golden anniversary be as special as the day you said "I do." Here's to many more years of love and laughter together.

New Baby

There's no greater miracle than the birth of a new baby.
Make new parents—or grandparents—happy by letting them know you understand
their feelings about this extraordinary event!

May God bless and keep that little miracle of yours.

May the joy of parenting bring you a lifetime of laughter and memories.

The miracle of life reveals itself in the tiny expressions of a newborn child. Congratulations on your miracle.

The sounds of baby feet will soon fill your home with unimaginable love and infectious laughter. Enjoy!

Congratulations! You have a brand-new reason to smile.

God has blessed you with a sweet little bundle of love.

When a child is born, parents are too. Congratulations on all of your birthdays!

What could be nicer than a new baby to love? Congratulations!

A baby is life's greatest blessing.

Girl or Boy

How perfect! A princess in pink to love and cherish. Congratulations!

A baby girl—how cute! May she fill your home with joy. Warmest wishes to you all.

Ribbons and bows and sweet baby toes.... Congratulations on the birth of your daughter!

Love, joy, happiness. Baby girls bring the best life has to give.

Baby boys are like angels that bounced from heaven.

A baby boy—how sweet! You must be so proud! Love and congratulations to all of you.

May your new baby boy open your eyes to all that's beautiful in life.

Religious Ceremonies

May the bond your baby forms with the Lord today guide him/her through a happy life. Happy christening day.

God bless your little bundle!

May your child always walk in the presence of angels.

May God bless your baby with his guidance on this baptism day, and bless your family with his love. Congratulations.

May you and your baby feel God's love today and always.

A grandchild blesses life with newfound youth and wonder. Congratulations.

Grandchild

Congratulations on your new grandchild! God has added a new love to your life.

Congratulations, Grandma! Your love will be an endless bridge across the generations.

Adoption

Congratulations on your new baby— specially chosen and doubly cherished!

God has touched your lives with love. Congratulations on your special baby.

You are so lucky to have found each other! Congratulations on the adoption of your new baby.

~

The most perfect gifts are those we give ourselves. Congratulations on your new baby!

Shower

~

May you find big doses of happiness in your little bundle of love.

Take time to remember this moment—on the baby's 18th birthday, today will feel like "just yesterday."

~

May God bless you and the family you've made.

~

Hope this shower is the start of a lifetime of rainbows for your baby!

Happy Holidays

Holidays are times of tradition, times of celebration.
They are the perfect opportunity to reach out to loved ones.

Christmas

Wishing you all the happy things this very special holiday brings!

'Tis the season to wrap the world in joy and love.

Wishing you a sleigh full of wishes and dreams come true.

May your heart be filled with every joy during this special time of year.

Wishing you and your family a Christmas frosted with winter magic.

This special season gives us a chance to renew our bonds with those we love. Have a wonderful holiday.

Christmases are like snowflakes: Each one is unique. May this holiday season be a memorable one.

May the spirit of the Christmas season fill you with joy.

Wishing you quiet moments with friends and family this holiday season, and peace and joy for the coming year.

May the magic and wonder of Christmas bless your home and bring you peace in the new year.

～

May the peace of Christmas renew your soul.

～

May love and happiness be yours in this season of joy.

～

Children building snow people, snow falling softly, Christmas lights twinkling—believe in the magic that is Christmas.

～

Hoping your days are filled with true friends, close family, and precious memories. Season's greetings.

May you have peace this Christmas and be guided by the strength of the Lord in the coming year.

～

Christmas is a special time of year, filled with peace, love, and thankfulness. Have a joyous season.

～

May Santa bring you joy this season and all year.

～

'Tis the season! Enjoy. Embrace. Celebrate. Merry Christmas.

～

Wishing you hot cocoa mornings and fireside nights this Christmas.

～

Christmas is God's gift to us. May its blessings bring you joy and peace the whole year through.

Hanukkah

May the candles in your window
spark peace around the world.
Happy Hanukkah!

May the blessings of Hanukkah
brighten your life.

A little light can go a long way toward
making the world a brighter place.
Happy Hanukkah!

May the remembrance of the eight-
day miracle bless your family with
hope and love.

May the Festival of Lights shine
bright with hope and happiness this
Hanukkah season.

Kwanzaa

May the principles of Kwanzaa offer
guidance and comfort to you and your
family.

May the joy of Kwanzaa touch you
and your family.

May this Kwanzaa season revitalize
unity for you and your family and
bring you peace and happiness.

May Kwanzaa carry your spirit high
this holiday season.

Celebrate culture and community,
family and future! Happy Kwanzaa!

Happy New Year

Wishing you a healthy, happy, and prosperous new year.

May God bless and keep you, now and throughout the year.

May the new year find you happy and surrounded by the love of family and friends. Happy New Year!

May this year be the best of your life so far!

Let the countdown to a memorable year begin! Happy New Year.

At this joyous time of year, keep friends and family close at hand.

Hoping your new year shines with peace, love, and happiness.

Hoping this year brings a bounty of blessings to you and yours.

Wishing you 365 chances to love, laugh, and live your best year yet.

Valentine's Day

You're the sun, the moon, and the stars in my life. Please be my valentine.

I found love, laughter, and life when I found you. Happy Valentine's Day!

Today is a special celebration of our love. Happy Valentine's Day!

~

My world is brighter now that you're in it, Valentine.

~

I'll keep it short and sweet: I love you.

~

A love like ours is a beautiful thing. Happy Valentine's Day.

~

I'm counting the minutes until I see you, my love.

~

Let's be honest—we were meant for each other.

~

You and me...that's all I need. Happy Valentine's Day.

I'd love to share my heart with you. Be my valentine.

~

The best gift I've ever received is you. Happy Valentine's Day.

~

My heart doesn't just beat for you—it soars! Happy Valentine's Day.

~

My life with you is better than I ever imagined it could be. Thank you for your love.

Mother's Day

Love, trust, friendliness, and courage
are some of the lessons you taught me.
What a great start you gave me in life!
I love you, Mom.

I am forever grateful for the gift of
you. Happy Mother's Day.

I just wanted to tell you how
important you are to me and how
much I love you. Happy Mother's Day.

My mother, my guide, my friend.
I love you.

I appreciate how hard you've worked
to make my life so good.
Thanks, Mom.

Father's Day

Thank you for years of wiping tears,
tucking in, cleaning cuts, making
dinner, making sacrifices, sharing
laughter, smiling, and just plain loving
me. Happy Father's Day!

From you I learned never to give up.
You're the best, Dad!

For all your sacrifices, all your advice,
and all your support, I love you.
Happy Father's Day.

You made my world a safe, happy place filled with love. Thanks, Dad.

I hope I'll be able to follow in your footsteps some day. You're a wonderful father, and I love you.

Easter

Wishing you a basket full of blessings this Easter!

May the blessings of this joyous season find their way into your home. Happy Easter.

May the Lord hear your prayers and touch you with love this Easter.

Though we can't be with you this Easter, we hold you dearly in our hearts.

God gave us the gift of life; may he find you enjoying it today and always. Happy Easter.

May the sacrifices the Lord made renew your joy and hope in life. Happy Easter.

Easter is a time for sharing blessings. Thank you for the blessing of our friendship. Hope you have a wonderful Easter.